Presented to

_____

On the occasion of

_____

From

_____

Date

_____

© 2000 by Barbour Publishing, Inc.

ISBN 1-57748-807-5

Scripture quotations are taken from the King James Version of the Bible.

The selection by Donna Lange is used with the author's permission.

Published by Barbour Publishing, Inc., P. O. Box 719, Uhrichsville, Ohio 44683 http://www.barbourbooks.com

Member of the
Evangelical Christian
Publishers Association

Printed in China.

An Invitation to Tea

A CELEBRATION OF TEA
& GOOD FRIENDS

Ellyn Sanna

BARBOUR
PUBLISHING, INC.

The cozy fire is bright and gay,

The merry kettle boils away

And burns a cheerful song.

I sing the saucer and the cup;

Pray, Mary, fill the teapot up,

And do not make it strong.

BARRY PAIN

Contents

1

AN ATMOSPHERE
OF INTIMACY

Somehow taking tea together encourages
an atmosphere of intimacy.
GAIL GRECO

Tea is the drink of friendship.

SARAH JANE EVANS AND GILES HILTON

. . .

In our hurried, impersonal world, we can be grateful for all the tiny rituals of intimacy that still exist. We experience one of these small, loving moments when we share cups of tea on a winter afternoon—or on a lazy, summer day, when we sip tall glasses of iced tea on a friend's front porch. These quiet moments of communion tie our hearts together—and whether we realize it or not, the caring acceptance we offer each other over cups of tea reveals to us God's face.

. . .

Every true friend is a glimpse of God.
LUCY LARCOM

MOMENTS OF LOVE
AND UNDERSTANDING

"I'll make tea," my friend Carolyn used to say to me, "and you can tell me all about it."

I'd sit at her kitchen table, back in the days before I had a family and home of my own, and, over cups of orange-spice tea, we would discuss my love life, my frustrations with my job, and my longings for the future. Somehow, I always came away with renewed hope, my focus on Christ's love a little clearer.

Today, years later, whenever I taste orange-spice tea, I still remember those moments of love and understanding at Carolyn's kitchen table.

The first cup of tea moistens my lips and throat;
the second cup breaks my loneliness.
LU T'UNG

. . .

Friends put the entire world to right

over a cup of tea.

CHARLOTTE GRAY

. . .

Friendship takes fear from the heart.
GEORGE ELIOT

CHINA SPOONS

After a hectic week, I seized the opportunity to be alone and escaped to the kitchen, while my husband entertained our three children. Moments later, one of my daughters discovered my hiding place.

"Mommy, do you want to have a tea party?"

"Sure," I replied, surprising myself.

She took my hand, and together we went to the china hutch. Her eyes sparkled as we selected delicate teacups and saucers. Her little hands gingerly placed my grandmother's Depression creamer on the table.

"We need china spoons, too," she said. She opened an old wooden box lined with green velvet, another heirloom, and chose two silver spoons. I poured milk into our teacups and sliced banana bread. With "china spoons," we scooped out chocolate and stirred it in our "tea." Then my daughter bowed her head.

"Dear Jesus, thank You that just Mommy and I are having a tea party. Amen."

We took dainty bites of bread and sipped our tea. I had thought I wanted to be alone, but now I savored our time together. A few minutes later, she skipped away.

I'm glad that as my daughter grows older, life will bring us many more opportunities to make treasured memories. One day, she'll be a woman; but when she is, I hope she will still invite me to join her for a cup of tea—served with china spoons, of course.

DONNA LANGE

A CUPFUL OF LOVE

Just six months ago, my eldest daughter still wanted to sit in my lap; on Sundays, she clung to me like a little limpet all through church, her head on my shoulder; and when we walked together across a parking lot, her hand would always reach for mine. These days, though, she's deep in the throes of adolescence; if I put my hand on her shoulder, she shrugs me off, like a horse that flicks away a fly with an irritated twitch. And I certainly know better now than to try to take her hand in any public place.

Sometimes I don't know how to tell her how much I still love her. If I say the words out loud, she usually rolls her eyes. But when she's cold, or sad, or feeling sick, I've discovered one thing she likes—she likes me to make her a cup of tea. Somehow that cup of steaming liquid shows her what she won't let me put in words: that I accept her growing independence and maturity, that I care about her troubles, and that I'm always here to listen if she needs me.

. . .

It is in the shelter of each other that people live.
IRISH PROVERB

11

Over cups of tea,
I listened to my friend,
and my friend heard me.
My joy was hers and hers was mine,
as we shared our hearts
line by line.

ANONYMOUS

. . .

The greatest gift we can give one another is
rapt attention to one another's existence.

SUE ATCHLEY EBAUGH

AN EVER-GROWING HARVEST

I'm not sure when my sister stopped being simply the beloved older sibling who always made me feel safe and special. Our friendship might have been born on a cold winter night while we talked over mugs of smoky Lapsang souchong tea; or it might have come to life one humid summer day when we laughed together on her back porch, with tall, brown glasses of iced tea on the table between us. Either way, I'm glad for all the moments of talk and tea we've shared.

I'm also grateful that on the cool, wet mountains of India and China, tea bushes will keep on growing, yielding their harvest of fragrant leaves— and over cups of that tea, the friendship my sister and I share will keep on growing, too, yielding a harvest of insight and comfort to us both.

. . .

What do we live for, if it is not to make life less difficult for each other?
GEORGE ELIOT

When I joined you for tea that rainy afternoon, my heart was as dreary as the sky. But cup by cup, the afternoon passed, while our conversation drove the clouds away from my heart. What's more, by that last cup of tea, my thoughts had been rearranged, leaving me space enough to breathe and light enough to see.

LUCIE CHRISTOPHER

. . .

I talked to friends
and found myself.

LOIS WYSE

2

ISLANDS OF STILLNESS

Teach me the art of
creating islands of stillness,
in which I can absorb the beauty
of everyday things. . . .

MARIAN STROUD

Like Elijah, too often all I can hear in my life is the noise of earthquakes and the roaring of fire. I hurry to meet my responsibilities, and all the while, my family changes around me as they grow older, my children encountering new emotional challenges, my parents facing the crises of poor health and aging. Too many earthquakes, too many fires. How can I possibly hope to hear God's "still, small voice"?

I can't get rid of the fire and earthquakes in my life. But I can choose to take a moment in even the busiest day, a tiny island of stillness when I sit in God's presence and simply sip my tea. Elaborate rituals and lengthy spiritual retreats are well and good in their place—but I don't need to wait for them to hear God's quiet voice. All I really need is a few deep breaths, the view from my kitchen window, and a cup of tea in my hands.

. . .

[Tea-drinking] is above all a comforting ritual, simultaneously soothing and stimulating, in which to withdraw momentarily from the busyness of our lives. . . .
ALEXANDRA STODDARD

Each cup of tea represents an imaginary voyage.
CATHERINE DOUZEL

. . .

The mere chink of cups

and saucers turns

the mind to happy repose.

GEORGE GISSING

. . .

Why should we live with such hurry and waste of life?
HENRY DAVID THOREAU

My friend Lois and I used to say to each other, "When life gets back to normal, we'll get together." Or ". . .we'll get our lives in shape" or ". . .we'll somehow make room for God's presence in our lives." The demands of Lois's job and church work, and the constant stress of a mother with Alzheimer's disease, make her life even more hectic than mine.

Finally, though, Lois said to me one day, "Let's face it. This is *normal* for us. We can't wait for our lives to slow down, for all the crises to end. We have to make time now. Want to meet for tea?"

I can control some of the craziness in my life, but some of it is truly beyond my control. I don't have to be a passive victim, though, pushed here and there by the world's frantic pace. Even on the most traumatic and stressful of days, God's serenity supports me.

I forget He's always there, though. That's why I need to remind myself by making time for friends, for peace, for quiet moments. . .for something as simple as a cup of tea.

. . .

As you make your tea, always linger a little over the moment. . .
enjoy the space and break from routine.
SARAH JANE EVANS AND GILES HILTON

3

HISTORY, TRADITION, AND FACTS

Thank God for tea!
What would the world do
without tea?—how did it exist?
I am glad I was not
born before tea.

REVEREND SYDNEY SMITH

WHAT IS TEA?

The tea plant is an evergreen shrub that grows in the mountains of China, northern India, and Malaysia, and in other mountainous areas where the weather is cool and rainy. It has fragrant white flowers, but the leaves are the parts that are picked, dried, and eventually packaged. Only the very tip of each branch will be used in the best teas, and it is picked by hand.

Tea plants are propagated from cuttings from a parent plant, thus assuring their "lineage." Within three years, the plants become productive and may continue to be for a century.

After tea leaves are "plucked," they are dried by "withering." This involves spreading leaves out for one full day on a wire-mesh frame covered with a thin cloth. Then the leaves are tossed in baskets to release their juices. The leaves ferment and begin to darken, releasing a pleasant fragrance much like apple blossoms. Then, to prevent further fermentation, the leaves are fired in a process similar to stir-frying, either in a wok or in large, industrial ovens. Last, the leaves are sorted into loose tea, broken leaves, or leaf dust, which is used in tea bags.

. . .

Better to be deprived of food for
three days, than tea for one.

ANCIENT CHINESE PROVERB

MEDICINAL USES FOR TEA

- Green tea may be used to soothe insect bites and to slow bleeding from cuts.
- Tea is said to boost the immune system and prevent tooth decay, because it is rich in fluoride.
- Oolong tea, sometimes called "dieter's tea," helps keep fats soluble in the body and supposedly helps lower blood cholesterol.
- Garlic tea is known for warding off colds.
- Chamomile tea is used to treat indigestion, insomnia, stress, and anxiety.
- Fennel tea is supposed to increase a mother's milk flow and relieve baby's colic.
- Meadowsweet tea was used to reduce fever and pain during Elizabethan times. In the early 1800s, anti-inflammatory chemicals called *salicylates* were extracted from meadowsweet tea. These chemicals were eventually reproduced in a synthetic form—aspirin—by the Bayer Pharmaceutical Company toward the end of the nineteenth century.
- Cold, wet tea bags make a soothing poultice for sties or tired eyes.

· · ·

So I must rise at early dawn, as busy as can be,
To get my daily labor done, and pluck the leafy tea.
LE YIH, 1644

THE HISTORY OF TEA

Circa 2700 B.C.　　Tea is discovered by Chinese Emperor Shen Nung.

Circa 725 B.C.　　Ch'a (Chinese ideograph for tea, which is a picture of a leaf) is introduced, showing importance of tea in daily life in China.

A.D. 805　　Tea is introduced into Japan.

1500　　First earthenware teapots are made in Yi-Xang, which is famous for its clay. Black, green, and oolong tea become popular.

1610　　The Dutch bring tea to Europe for the first time, purchased from Chinese merchants who speak the Amoy dialect, and assign to the beverage their word "tea."

1773　　King George levies a tax on tea in the American colonies, and the colonists respond by throwing a cargo load of tea into the Boston harbor—the Boston Tea Party.

1840s	Anna, the seventh Duchess of Bedford, begins the English institution known as "afternoon tea." The Duchess of Bedford often had a "sinking feeling" in the afternoon, because lunch was usually only a few snacks, and dinner was not served until eight o'clock—so she begins inviting friends for tea and cakes at five o'clock.
1904	At the St. Louis World's Fair in 1904, Richard Blechynden, a tea merchant, introduces some little known teas to the public. Because of the intense heat, no one is much interested in drinking hot tea, so Mr. Blechynden throws in a few ice cubes. Iced tea is an instant success.
1908	Thomas Sullivan, another American tea merchant, stumbles onto tea bags after providing samples of his teas to clients in little, stitched silk sachets.
20th century	Tea is second only to water as the world's most popular and least expensive drink. Each day, over three billion cups of tea are consumed.

DIFFERENT TYPES OF TEAS

Tea is separated into three categories: Black, green, and oolong. Black and oolong teas are rolled, withered, fermented to varying degrees, and dried, while green teas are only rolled and dried. These popular teas are all black teas:

Assam	Darjeeling	Nilgiri
Ceylon	Keemum	Lapsang souchong

In addition to tea plants, tea may be made using any number of the leaves, roots, or flowers of other plants to create "tisanes," or herbal teas. These may include:

Basil	Catnip	Chamomile
Chicory	Chrysanthemum	Ginger
Ginseng	Jasmine	Lavender
Lemon Verbena	Licorice	Lime
Peppermint	Red Raspberry	Strawberry
	Blackberry	

THE HISTORY OF TEA PREFERENCES AROUND THE WORLD

* When tea was first shipped to Europe, small, handleless cups and saucers with bowls and covers came with it. To accommodate European preference, China began to produce cups with handles. When tea prices dropped, the cups grew larger.
* Russians preferred drinking their tea "with their eyes" from glass cups, to make it a visual experience as well as one for the palate.
* By the end of Queen Victoria's sixty-year reign, tea drinking had become a national pastime. Victoria's favorite sweet to eat with tea was sponge cake served with a layer of strawberry jam and whipped cream. She returned from visiting her eldest daughter in Russia with the new custom of drinking tea with a slice of lemon, which also quickly became popular.
* Today in England, tea is more than a tradition; it is a way of life. Great Britain is the largest tea-consuming nation in the world.
* "High tea" is still served in the North of England in the late afternoon and may consist of cold meats, salad, cakes, fruits, scrambled eggs, and bacon—as well as tea.
* In many Arab countries, tea is the first sign of friendship. It is served with intensely sweet pastries.

TEA PARTY RECIPES

Come oh come ye tea-thirsty restless ones—
the kettle boils, bubbles, and sings,
musically.
RABINDRANATH TAGORE

DIFFERENT KINDS OF TEA

VANILLA MILK TEA

This is a sweet, milky tea which works well for introducing children to the drink.

    1 cup milk
    1 2-inch piece of vanilla bean, split
        (if available; otherwise 2 tsp of pure vanilla extract)
    4 tsp English Breakfast Tea
    1 quart boiling water

Simmer milk and the vanilla bean in a small saucepan, stirring often. Remove from heat and allow to stand until milk is cool. Remove vanilla bean. Ready teapot and teacups with hot water, drain and dry. Place tea leaves in teapot and add boiling water. Cover with a tea towel and steep for 5 minutes. Pour ¼ cup of cold milk into teacups. Strain tea into hot cups and serve. Yields 4 to 5 servings.

HOT CITRUS TEA

2 cups water
6 whole cloves
1½ quarts of water
8 tea bags

½ cup lemon juice
⅔ cup orange juice
1½ cups sugar

Combine 2 cups water and cloves in a saucepan and bring to a boil. Remove from heat and let stand 2 hours. Bring 1½ quarts water to boil and add tea bags. Remove from heat, cover, and let stand for 5 minutes. Remove tea bags. Strain clove mixture and add to tea. Add fruit juice and sugar, stirring until sugar dissolves. Let stand 1 hour. Reheat when ready to serve. Yields 2 quarts.

. . .

Its taste is perhaps the subtlest the tongue can experience,
so unassertive it can be almost subliminal.
Tea both calms and stimulates,
but its secret teaching is conscious enjoyment.
NORWOOD PRATT

RUSSIAN TEA

1 cup sugar
1 cup water
25 whole cloves
1 quart weak tea

juice of 1 lemon
juice of 2 oranges
pinch of salt

Combine sugar, water, and cloves; simmer for 20 minutes. Add to tea and fruit juice. Add pinch of salt.

. . .

There is a great deal of poetry and fine sentiment in a chest of tea.
RALPH WALDO EMERSON

. . .

Ecstacy is a glass full of tea.
ALEXANDER PUSHKIN

CHRISTMAS FRUIT TEA

2 quarts cranberry juice
1 (46 ounce) can pineapple juice
1 (6 ounce) can frozen concentrated lemonade, thawed
2 cups apple juice
1 cup orange juice
4 sticks of cinnamon
3 whole nutmegs
1½ tsps ground ginger

Pour first 5 ingredients into a 30-cup electric coffee percolator. Place spices in percolator basket. Perk through complete cycle; let stand 1 hour. Serve hot. Yields 1 gallon.

. . .

*Tea. . .will always be
the favored beverage of
the intellectual.*

THOMAS DE QUINCY

TEA BREADS AND SWEETS
FOR EATING WITH TEA

MOIST APPLE-WALNUT BREAD

½ cup (1 stick) unsalted butter
¾ cup granulated sugar
2 large whole eggs
2 large McIntosh apples, peeled and grated
½ cup chopped walnuts
1 tsp pure vanilla extract
1¾ cups unbleached all-purpose flour
½ tsp salt
1 tsp baking soda
1 tsp baking powder

Preheat the oven to 350 degrees. Grease a 4½ x 8½-inch loaf pan and set aside. With an electric mixer, cream the butter and sugar until light and fluffy. Add eggs, one at a time, beating well after each addition. Combine apples, walnuts, and vanilla. Fold apple mixture into the butter mixture and stir well to combine. Sift dry ingredients together and gradually add to the wet ingredients, stirring well to combine. Pour the batter into the greased loaf pan and bake in a preheated oven for 1 hour, or until toothpick inserted in the center comes out clean. Cool, unmold, and slice to serve. Makes one 8½-inch loaf.

BUTTERMILK SCONES

5 cups unbleached all-purpose flour
1 cup granulated sugar
1 tsp salt
2 tbsps plus ½ tsp baking powder
2 tsps baking soda
2 tbsps solid shortening
½ cup unsalted butter
2 whole eggs
1½ cups buttermilk
1½ cups raisins, currants, or blueberries
1 egg white

Preheat oven to 450 degrees. Sift together all dry ingredients in a large mixing bowl. Gently rub shortening and butter into the flour mixture with your fingers. Mixture should have the appearance of wet sand. Add eggs, one at a time, and then buttermilk, being sure to mix well after each addition. Coat raisins with flour and add to the dough. Knead the dough fifteen turns and then form into a 10 x 10 x 2-inch square on a well-floured surface. Divide dough into 24 small squares. Place on two large baking sheets, two inches apart, and brush with egg white. Bake in preheated oven for 20 minutes or until lightly brown, with scones retaining their square shape. Cool on baking sheets for several minutes, then serve warm. Makes 2 dozen tea scones.

BERRY TEA MUFFINS

2 whole eggs, beaten
½ cup whole milk
¼ cup (½ stick) unsalted butter, melted
2 cups unbleached all-purpose flour
1 tbsp baking powder
½ teaspoon salt
½ cup granulated sugar
1 cup blueberries, raspberries, or other berries

Preheat oven to 400 degrees. Insert paper cupcake holders in twenty-four 2-inch muffin tins. Beat eggs with an electric mixer until foamy, then stir in milk and butter. Sift dry ingredients and fold into wet mixture, stirring just to blend; do not overmix. Gently fold the berries into batter. Pour batter into muffin tins and bake in preheated oven for 12 minutes, or until muffins are lightly browned. Cool for a few minutes, then turn out onto a wire rack and serve while still warm. Makes 2 dozen tea muffins.

TINY PECAN PIES

3 ounces cream cheese
½ cup (1 stick) plus 1 tbsp unsalted butter, softened
1 cup sifted unbleached all-purpose flour
1 whole egg
¾ cup brown sugar
1 tsp pure vanilla extract
pinch of salt
⅔ cup chopped pecans

Preheat oven to 325 degrees. Blend cream cheese and ½ cup butter with an electric mixer in a large mixing bowl. Gradually add flour, beating well after each addition. Separate dough into twenty-four 1-inch balls and press into bottom and along sides of twenty-four ungreased 2-inch muffin tins. In another bowl, beat egg with an electric mixer until foamy. Gradually add brown sugar, remaining 1 tbsp of butter, vanilla, and salt, beating well after each addition. Sprinkle half of the pecans into the pastry-lined muffin tins. Divide egg filling evenly among the tins, and sprinkle remaining pecans over the top of the filling. Bake in preheated oven for 25 minutes, or until filling is firm and pastry light brown. Cool completely and serve. Makes twenty-four 2-inch pies.

LEMON BREAD

2 cups all-purpose flour
1 tbsp baking powder
¼ tsp salt
½ cup (1 stick) butter, softened
1 cup sugar

2 eggs
grated zest of 1 lemon
1 tsp lemon extract
¾ cup lemonade

Preheat oven to 350 degrees. Grease and flour a 9 x 5 x 3-inch loaf pan. Place wax paper in bottom of pan and grease and flour also, shaking out any excess flour. Thoroughly stir together flour, baking powder, and salt in medium-sized bowl. In a separate bowl, beat butter and sugar until light and fluffy, scraping sides of bowl often. Add eggs, one at a time, beating well after each addition. Add lemon zest and lemon extract. At low speed, add dry mixture to butter mixture alternately with lemonade until just blended. Spread batter evenly in pan. Bake for 60 to 65 minutes or until a toothpick inserted in center of loaf comes out clean. Cool in pan on a wire rack for 10 minutes. Then remove from pan and peel off wax paper, allowing bread to cool completely on wire rack. Yields one 9-inch loaf.

CINNAMON RAISIN ROLL-UPS

Similar to old-fashioned cinnamon toast, this goes well served with Vanilla Milk Tea.

12 thin slices white bread
6 tbsps (¾ stick) butter, softened
½ cup sugar

1½ tbsps cinnamon
½ cup raisins

Preheat oven to 300 degrees. Remove crusts from bread. Lightly roll each slice with rolling pin to make thinner. In a medium-sized bowl, cream butter and sugar; then stir in cinnamon. Spread butter mixture equally over bread slices. Make a row of raisins along one side of each slice of bread. Beginning with this side, roll each slice up like a jelly roll. Secure with a toothpick. Place roll-ups on an ungreased cookie sheet, seam side down, and toast in oven until lightly browned, turning regularly to brown all sides. Serve warm. Yields 12 roll-ups.

NORTHUMBERLAND
"SINGIN' HINNY"

4 tbsps butter
2½ cups self-rising flour
1 tsp salt

4 tbsps superfine sugar
6 tbsps currants
¾ cup half-and-half

Sift flour and sugar into a large mixing bowl and cut softened butter into mixture. Stir in sugar and currants. Making a well in the center, pour in the half-and-half. Gently fold the dry ingredients into the liquid to make a soft dough. Roll the dough to about ¼-inch thick on a lightly-floured surface and prick all over with a fork. Cut into four pieces and cook on a medium/hot griddle for about four minutes per side or until nicely browned. Serve while still hot, cut in two, and buttered.

NOTE: "Hinny" is a term of endearment English mothers used for their children—and "singin' " is the term used to describe the sound the cakes made as they cooked. When children asked impatiently if their tea and cakes were ready to eat, their mothers would tell them that they were not ready yet, "just singin' hinny."

SPREADS FOR TEA BREADS

GINGER-FLAVORED HONEY

Ginger became a very important spice in England after trade began between Europe and the Orient. Its flavor makes a nice complement to honey's sweetness.

2 cups (16 ounces) light-colored honey
½ cup chopped candied ginger

Stir honey over medium heat until thoroughly warmed. Stir in ginger. Pour mixture into a heat-proof jar and cover. Let mixture cool to room temperature before serving. Yields 2 cups.

ORANGE HONEY

Because of the zesty nature of this spread, pick a full-bodied honey such as clover or alfalfa honey as the base.

1 cup (8 ounces) honey   grated zest of 1 orange

Stir honey over medium heat until warmed through. Add orange zest and stir. Pour mixture into a heat-proof jar and cover and allow to cool before serving. Yields 1 cup.

BERRY-FLAVORED HONEY

This honey is especially suited to breads, scones, or muffins. Prepare it when berries are in season so it may be enjoyed during the cold winter months.

    2 cups (16 ounces) light-colored honey
    ½ cup fresh raspberries or strawberries

Stir honey in small saucepan over medium heat until warm. Add berries and stir gently. Pour honey into a heat-proof jar and bring to room temperature. Cover tightly and allow honey to stand at room temperature for 3 days before refrigerating.

STRAWBERRY BUTTER

½ cup (1 stick) butter, softened   ½ cup fresh strawberries,
2 to 3 tbsps confectioners' sugar   washed and hulled

Divide butter into 6 to 8 pieces and place in food processor with strawberries. While processing butter and strawberries, add confectioners' sugar until butter is smooth and even-colored. If mixing by hand, cream butter and sugar, and mix mashed strawberries (a fork will do) with butter mixture. Yields 1 cup.

HOW TO BREW
A PERFECT CUP OF TEA

- Use a clean, warmed, well-seasoned teapot.
- Add a tea bag (or one teaspoon of tea leaves) for each 6-ounce cup of tea.
- Bring fresh, cold water to a boil and pour over the tea leaves.
- Cover and let tea brew for three to five minutes.
- Stir once and promptly remove tea bag or pour liquid off leaves.
- Sit back, relax, enjoy!

. . .

If you are cold, tea will warm you;
if you are too heated, it will cool you;
if you are depressed, it will cheer you;
if you are exhausted, it will calm you.
WILLIAM GLADSTONE